KU-467-067

KEEPING HEALTHY
Harmful Substances

Text by Carol Ballard
Photography by Robert Pickett

HODDER
Wayland

an imprint of Hodder Children's Books

TITLES IN THE KEEPING HEALTHY SERIES:

• Personal Hygiene • Eating • Safety
• Exercise • Relationships • Harmful Substances

© 2004 White-Thomson Publishing Ltd

Produced by White-Thomson Publishing Ltd
2/3 St Andrew's Place, Lewes, BN7 1UP

Editor: Elaine Fuoco-Lang

Consultant: Chris Sculthorpe, East Sussex,
                     Brighton & Hove Healthy
                     School Scheme Co-ordinator

Inside design: Joelle Wheelwright

Cover design: Hodder Wayland

Photographs: Robert Pickett

Proofreader: Jane Colgan

Artwork: Peter Bull

Published in Great Britain in 2004 by Hodder
Wayland, an imprint of Hodder Children's Books.
Hodder Children's Books, a division of
Hodder Headline Limited, 338 Euston Road,
London, NW1 3BH.

The right of Carol Ballard to be identified as the
author of this Work has been asserted by her in
accordance with the Copyright, Designs and Patents
Act 1988.

All rights reserved. No part of this publication may
be reproduced, stored in a retrieval system, or
transmitted, in any form or by any means without
the prior written permission of the publisher, nor be
otherwise circulated in any form of binding or
cover other than that in which it is published and
without a similar condition being imposed on the
subsequent purchaser.

British Library Cataloguing in Publication Data
Ballard, Carol
    Harmful substances. - (Keeping Healthy)
    1. Substance abuse - Juvenile literature
    I. Title
    613.8
ISBN 0 7502 4341 4

Printing and binding at C&C China.

Acknowledgements:
The publishers would like to thank the following
for their assistance with this book: the staff
and children of Salmestone Primary School,
Margate, Kent.

Picture acknowledgements:
Angela Hampton Family Picture Library 4, 5 top, 9
top, 13 top, 15 top, 18 bottom, 20 bottom, 21 bottom,
22 top, 28; CORBIS 10 bottom, 13 bottom, 14 top, Jeff
Albertson 23 bottom, Andrew Brookes 22 bottom,
Jim Cummins 29 top; Robert Essel NYC 18 top, Paul
Hardy 19 top, Richard Hutchings 17 top, Julius 16
top, Ronnie Kaufman 20 top and 29 bottom, Lester
Lefkowiz 25 top, Roy Morsch 23 top, Mug Shots 26
top, Anna Palma 19 bottom, Steve Starr 25 bottom,
Eye Ubiquitous 24 top; Hodder Wayland Picture
Library 8 top, 11 top, 12 bottom, 27; Robert Pickett 6
top, 8 bottom, 9 bottom, 10 top, 11 bottom, 14
bottom, 17 bottom, 21 top, 24 bottom; Simon Fraser/
Science Photo Library 12 top; WTPix 5 bottom, 6
bottom, 15 bottom.

The photographs in this book are of models
who have granted their permission for their use
in this title.

Contents

What are harmful substances?

It is good to know that our homes, schools and other places we may go are safe and that we are unlikely to come to any harm. All around us, though, are things that could hurt us. Most of the time we are protected from them, but there are times when you need to be responsible for your own safety and know what to do to look after yourself.

▲ *We usually feel safe at home with our families.*

There are many different types of harmful substances. Some, such as cleaning materials, are everyday things that many people have in their homes. You may see adults using others, such as alcohol and cigarettes; they may seem safe, but there can be hidden dangers. Medicines may be harmful if taken in the wrong amounts and by the wrong people. Other harmful substances include drugs that you may have heard about such as cannabis, ecstasy, heroin and cocaine.

▲ *Alcohol can be harmful if used unwisely.*

▼ *Knowing about the possible dangers can help you to make sensible decisions that will keep you healthy and safe.*

Everyday substances

Most people keep a range of different cleaning materials, such as bleach and disinfectant, in their homes. These are very useful but they can make you very ill if you swallow them. Some can also cause nasty burns if they touch your skin, and some give off fumes that can hurt your lungs and make it difficult to breathe. Do not use substances like this unless an adult has told you to, and always read the safety warnings on the label.

▲ **Oven cleaner contains chemicals that can cause harm if the product is used incorrectly.**

Many people use chemicals in the garden. Weedkillers will not only kill weeds, they also give you a very bad stomach ache if you swallow them, and you may need a trip to hospital. Other substances such as insect sprays and fertilisers are bad for you too, so stay well away.

▲ **An organic garden does not use any chemicals.**

If you do accidentally swallow something you shouldn't or spill something on your skin, tell an adult straight away. They can make sure you get the help and first aid that you need.

▶ **Emergency services, such as this ambulance in Sweden, can help to provide treatment on board their vehicle.**

\!?/ Fantastic Facts

It makes sense to keep substances that could harm people in their original containers. Special signs on bottles and other containers act as a code to tell people whether the contents are dangerous or not. Some of the signs are:

● a skull and cross-bones means 'POISON'

● a flame means 'will easily catch fire'

● an X means 'will irritate skin'.

Tankers carrying chemicals have these signs on them, so that if there is an accident and the contents are spilled, the emergency services know how to deal with it safely.

Medicines

Medicines are substances that are taken to help your body to recover from illness. All medicines are drugs: substances that, when they enter your body, have an effect on you or on the way you feel. Medicines can be very powerful and, if not taken properly, can be dangerous. Whenever a doctor writes a prescription, he or she makes sure that the medicine is correct for their patient. The medicine itself, or the amount of it, may be totally wrong and possibly harmful for someone else. Never ever be tempted to take somebody else's medicine, even if it looks exactly the same as your own. Medicines always have information about how much should be taken, and how often.

▲ *If you are unsure about how to take your medicine, always ask an adult.*

There may be instructions about when to take it, such as before or after a meal, just before you go to bed or when you first wake up. It is important to follow all these instructions carefully so that the medicine can work properly.

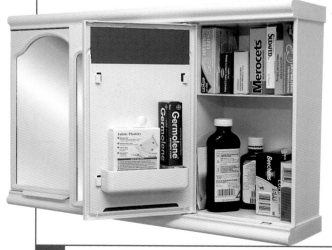

◄ *This cabinet has a lock on it so that when it is closed, young children cannot reach the medicines and take them by accident.*

Not all drugs are medicines, though. Some drugs affect your body and the way you feel, but they harm your body rather than helping it. This includes some common substances such as nicotine and alcohol, as well as other more dangerous substances.

Some everyday things like coffee and chocolate can also affect your body and how you feel, so really they are drugs. Unless you consume huge amounts, though, they are unlikely to do you any harm.

◀ *Even chocolate can affect how you feel.*

 # Healthy Hints

Sometimes, we may take medicines when we do not actually need them. This is not a good idea, as our bodies may get used to them so that when we are really ill they do not work as well. Often, if you feel unwell, perhaps with a tummy ache or a headache, a quiet rest will do as much good as a tablet or other medicine.

▲ *If you feel unwell, resting is often a good idea.*

Smoking

People smoke for many different reasons. For some, smoking is a habit that they have had for many years and cannot break. Some young people start to smoke to copy other people in their families. Others are persuaded to start by friends who are smokers. Some young people think that smoking makes them look grown up, or helps them to become part of a group.

▲ **Smoking is harmful to your body whatever your age.**

Cigarettes are made from the crushed, dried leaves of tobacco plants, held together by a strip of paper. Some have a plug of material, called a filter, at one end. As they burn, the leaves produce chemicals and gases.

◀ **The leaves from tobacco plants are used to make cigarettes.**

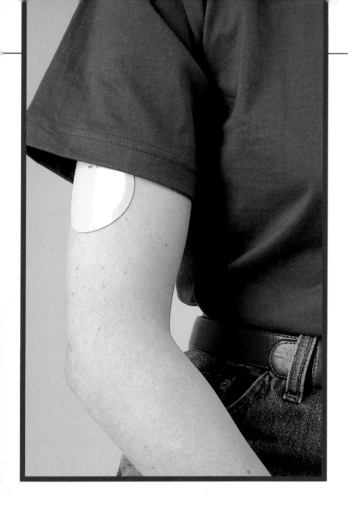

Smokers become addicted to nicotine, one of the chemicals produced when tobacco is burnt. This means that they need to keep smoking to keep getting more nicotine.

Scientists have tried to find ways to make it easier to give up smoking. Some patches to stick on the skin release tiny amounts of nicotine into the body. This is just enough to stop the person wanting another cigarette. Chewing gum that contains nicotine can also help.

◄ *A nicotine patch can help a person to give up smoking.*

 Healthy Hints

Many smokers find that they become very irritable when they try to give up their cigarettes, and often feel nervous and anxious. Some eat a lot of sweets instead, and some find that they start to put on weight. It makes good sense never to start smoking because then you'll never have to battle to give it up!

► *Nicotine in cigarettes makes smoking difficut to give up.*

How does smoking harm your body?

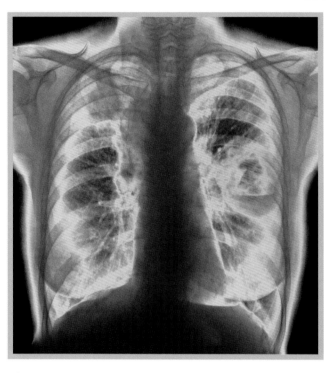

▲ *This x-ray shows that smoking has caused this person to develop lung cancer.*

Nicotine is a chemical produced when tobacco is burnt. It is addictive, which means that it acts as a drug and smokers find it hard to live without it. They say that it helps them to relax and stay calm. It may do these things – but it has other effects too. Nicotine makes the heart beat more quickly. It makes the blood vessels narrower so the heart has to work harder to pump the blood around the body. Nicotine also makes the stomach produce more acid, which can lead to stomach ulcers.

Burning tobacco also produces a sticky brown liquid called tar. This gets into the lungs when you breathe in cigarette smoke. It can clog up the narrow passages in the lungs, making breathing difficult. It can also damage the lungs themselves, causing diseases such as lung cancer.

▶ *Tar that collects in your lungs if you smoke.*

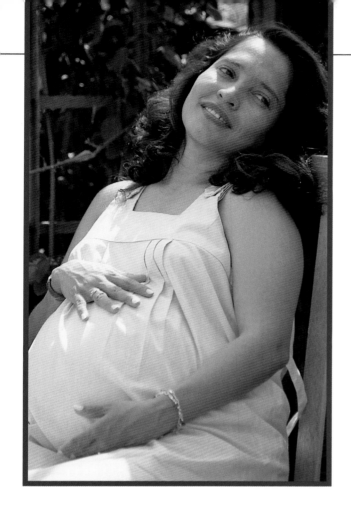

Cigarette smoke can make you look and smell unpleasant. Yellow-stained fingers, yellow-tinged hair, wrinkly skin, brown teeth, bad breath: all of these are unattractive, and they can all result from smoking cigarettes.

If a woman smokes while she is pregnant, it can harm her unborn baby. Babies born to mothers who smoke are more likely to be underweight and suffer from infections than babies born to non-smoking mothers.

◀ *This mother-to-be is wise not to smoke because smoking can harm everyone, including unborn children.*

¡?¡ Fantastic Facts

Have you ever looked across a room filled with the smoky haze of cigarette smoke? Even if you don't smoke, sitting in a smoky room means that the air you breathe in contains some of the chemicals and gases produced from burning cigarettes. This is called passive smoking. Scientists and doctors are beginning to realise that passive smoking causes illness in non-smokers just as cigarettes cause illness in smokers.

▶ *No smoking areas are becoming increasingly common.*

Alcohol

Alcohol is a drug that many people say makes them feel relaxed, happy and confident. Lots of adults enjoy drinking alcohol and, drunk sensibly and in small quantities, it will not harm them. Many, though, drink too much alcohol too often, and this can cause a lot of damage to their bodies.

▶ *Drinking in moderation with friends can be fun.*

There is a wide variety of alcoholic drinks. Beer, lager, wine, cider and spirits such as vodka, gin and brandy all contain alcohol. They do not all contain the same amount of alcohol though: some are much, much stronger than others. The amount of alcohol is measured in 'units'. Although doctors may give advice about the maximum number of units a person can drink in a week without affecting their health, the safer choice is to avoid alcohol altogether.

◀ *Spirits such as whisky and vodka contain much more alcohol than beers and lagers.*

Some drinks can be misleading. They may look like ordinary juices and fizzy drinks but they can contain a lot of alcohol. It might seem like a good idea to try them, but it is better to avoid them.

► *It is better for you to have a soft drink than one containing alcohol.*

!?/ Fantastic Facts

Many people drink alcohol, but there are strict laws controlling who can sell it, buy it and drink it, and when and where it can be sold, bought and drunk. In Britain, it is illegal for a shopkeeper to sell alcohol to anyone under 18, and in America the rules about age vary from one state to another. In some countries, alcohol is banned completely.

◄ *You don't need to drink alcohol to have a great time.*

Alcohol and behaviour

Alcohol is often thought to cheer you up, but the drug really slows the body down so that you begin to lose control. There is a delay of just a few minutes between drinking alcohol and the alcohol reaching the brain. At first, it may produce a feeling of happiness and relaxation. As more is consumed, the heart beats faster. Vision, speech and balance are all affected and the person seems 'drunk'. The person slowly loses control and may do things that they would never dream of doing normally. They may be very ashamed and embarrassed about their behaviour later.

▲ *It can be tempting to drink lots with your friends but this can make you act differently and make you feel unwell.*

Lots of trouble can be caused by groups of teenage boys and girls who have drunk too much lager or other alcohol. They are noisy, behave badly and may be in trouble with the police for upsetting other people or for damaging cars, buildings and other things. The results of what may have begun as an evening's fun can be serious and long-term.

◀ This police officer in Florida is checking that this driver has not been drinking by watching him walk along a line on the road. If you have been drinking, your balance becomes affected.

〰 Action Zone

Laws about drinking alcohol and driving may vary from one country to another, but scientists everywhere agree that drinking alcohol slows your reaction to things that happen around you. Test your reaction time:

1. Ask a friend to hold a ruler in the air, with '30cm' at the top.

2. Without actually touching the ruler, hold your thumb and first finger at the '0' . . . watch carefully . . . when they let go, try to catch it as quickly as you can. Read the number to see how many centimetres the ruler fell before you caught it.

The smaller the number, the faster your reaction time.

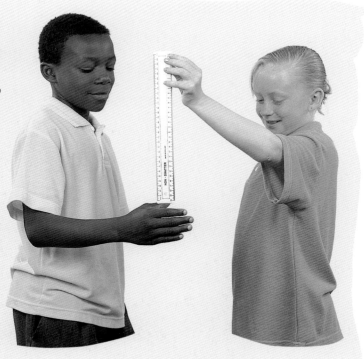

▲ How quick are your reactions? Reaction times are very important when driving which is why people shouldn't drink and drive.

How does alcohol harm your body?

Alcohol affects your body in several ways. Some effects are swift while others take longer to develop. Alcohol slows down the messages passing between the brain and the rest of the body so that it becomes harder to control speech, vision and balance. Alcohol irritates the lining of the stomach, causing nausea and vomiting. Excess alcohol may cause a person to lose consciousness and, in extreme cases, alcohol poisoning may lead to death.

▲ *Drinking too much alcohol can make you feel unwell.*

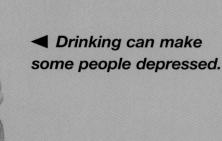

◀ *Drinking can make some people depressed.*

After drinking a lot of alcohol, a person may suffer from a hangover the next day. This usually means feeling tired, together with sickness and a bad headache.

Drinking too much over a long period can have a bad effect on a person's health. Alcohol is high in calories so many heavy drinkers are fat and overweight. The blood pressure may be raised and heart muscle damaged. The brain may also deteriorate. The liver removes alcohol from the blood, but too much alcohol can cause damage to the liver itself, leaving it enlarged and scarred. Continued heavy drinking can lead to liver failure and death.

▲ *Overeating as well as heavy drinking can cause obesity.*

!?/ Fantastic Facts

If a woman drinks alcohol while she is pregnant, it may harm her unborn baby. The alcohol in the mother's blood can pass to the baby, slowing down the rate at which it grows. Alcohol may also damage the baby's brain, and may stop others organs, such as the eyes, developing properly.

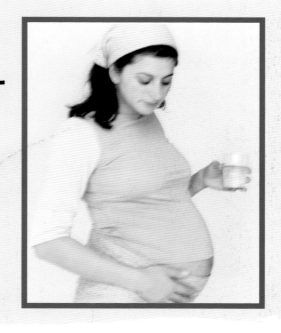

▶ *Pregnant women should avoid alcohol.*

Solvents

Have you ever noticed the distinctive smell as you pass a dry cleaners? That is an example of a solvent smell. Solvents are chemicals that give off strong gases.

▶ **Solvents are used when clothes are dry cleaned.**

Many solvents are used in substances such as glues, lighter fuel, cleaning fluids and some aerosols.

They can be used safely for their intended purpose, as long as the safety precautions are followed carefully. Used wrongly though, solvents can kill.

◀ **Solvents are used in correction fluid. Always use correction fluid in a well ventilated area.**

!?! Fantastic Facts

Shops that sell glue and similar products have signs saying that it is illegal to sell solvents to children and teenagers. The age limits may vary from one country to another, but the penalties for shops that break the law in this way are usually strict and severe. This is because governments all recognise how very dangerous solvents can be.

▶ *All of these products are dangerous if you don't use them for what they were designed for.*

Some people 'sniff' solvents. This is extremely dangerous. A single cigarette or alcoholic drink is unlikely to kill you, but just one whiff of a solvent might. 'Glue sniffers' inhale the gas from solvents because they like the feeling of light-headedness and dizziness that it gives them. Some say it makes them feel happy and excited. Some even squirt the solvent into their mouths. NEVER be tempted to try either of these. You can die almost immediately from heart failure or suffocation.

◀ *Some people get others to buy solvents for them. Don't be tempted to buy solvents to 'sniff' them because this is very dangerous.*

Ecstasy and cannabis

Ecstasy is a drug that is becoming increasingly used by young people, especially at places such as nightclubs. It is also known as 'E' or 'XTC'.

Ecstasy is usually taken as a tablet. People say it makes them feel very happy and more aware of what is happening around them than usual. They may also feel warm and friendly towards other people.

▲ *Even if people you know take drugs, you should never feel you have to do the same.*

As with any illegal drug, though, you cannot be sure just what it contains. The tablets may contain a very large amount of the drug. They may also contain other chemicals. Either of these could be very dangerous and possibly even kill you. Newspapers regularly tell stories of young people who died after taking just one Ecstasy tablet.

◄ *Ecstasy tablets are a dangerous drug.*

Cannabis has a lot of other names, including pot, marijuana, hash, grass and dope. It is made from the dried leaves of the cannabis plant and looks like dried grass. Most people who use it roll it up and smoke it like a cigarette. The juice and leaves of the cannabis plant can also be used and baked with food. People who use cannabis say it helps them to relax and calm down. However, using cannabis can make it harder to do well at school, as it may affect your concentration, your memory and your ability to get yourself to the right place at the right time. Although using cannabis is unlikely to kill you, it can cause problems in your everyday life. Some scientists think that using cannabis may lead to mental health problems.

▲ *Cannabis is made from the leaves of a cannabis plant.*

⟨?⟩ Fantastic Facts

Some people think that doctors should be allowed to prescribe cannabis as a medicine for particular patients. People suffering from diseases such as multiple sclerosis often find that cannabis can help to control the symptoms of their illness and make them feel much better. In the United Kingdom, though, using cannabis is still illegal.

► *A wheelchair-bound member of The Cannabis Club, in the US, holding a pipe for smoking prescribed medicinal marijuana.*

Heroin and cocaine

Heroin is made from opium poppy plants. It can be smoked, but is more usually injected. People say it makes them feel warm and comfortable, but there can be unpleasant side effects such as sickness and headaches.

Heroin is known by many different names, including smack, skag and junk. It is usually found as a white or brown powder. It is illegal to use heroin in many countries, including Britain and the US.

► *Poppies can be used to make opium.*

One of the main problems with heroin is that it is addictive. This means that once a person has used it, they are likely to want to use it again. They become used to it and then find it very difficult to live without regular injections of the drug. Heroin is very expensive so many people end up stealing and getting involved with other crimes in order to pay for it.

▼ *Needles that have been used before are not safe.*

Heroin users often share needles when injecting the drug. They may also use needles that have been used before and may not be sterile. This means that diseases can easily be passed from one person to another.

▲ *Cocaine is a very addictive drug.*

Cocaine is a white crystalline substance. It has several other names, including coke, snow and stardust. People who use cocaine say it makes them feel alert and very happy. Afterwards, though, they often feel sad and nervous.

Cocaine is usually taken by sniffing it into the nostrils. It is very addictive, so once a person takes cocaine they are likely to want more and more. Sniffing cocaine slowly destroys the inside of the nose, leaving the face disfigured and ugly.

Crack cocaine is a very strong, very pure form of cocaine and is even more dangerous than ordinary cocaine. It is usually taken by smoking.

\!?/ Fantastic Facts

Opium poppies are grown abroad and the heroin they produce is smuggled into other countries. Cocaine is often smuggled from one country to another as well. Police and other officials from different countries work together to try to stop the trade. The laws in most countries mean there are long prison sentences and, in some places, even execution for people involved in smuggling heroin and cocaine.

▲ *This official is using a sniffer dog to check that this cargo does not contain any illegal drugs.*

What is addiction?

Addiction means needing something and not being able to give it up. A drug addict is unable to manage without regular doses of a drug, even though they may know they are harming themselves by taking it.

▲ **Drug addiction can result in a lot of trouble.**

Addiction can really mess up a person's life. Most drugs damage the body in some way and many affect the mind as well. Addicts often skip school, college and other important things so they end up doing less well than other people. Many addicts cannot afford the drugs they need so they steal to make enough money to pay for them. They often find themselves in trouble with the police.

Healthy Hints

It can be difficult to know what to do if you are offered something you don't want to take. Here are some suggestions:

● Stay cool, calm and confident – say 'No', and stick to it.

● Keep repeating the same answer, e.g. 'I don't take drugs'.

● Ignore the offer – talk about something else.

● If they start to taunt you, avoid arguing – say something like 'O.K.' or 'Whatever'.

● Tell an adult you trust all about it as soon as you can.

Having an addict in the family is very difficult for everybody. The addict's behaviour may make the rest of the family feel awkward, embarrassed or ashamed. Parents may want to help but be at a loss to know what to do. Younger brothers and sisters can be upset and influenced by the addict's behaviour and attitudes.

► Taking drugs may make you feel happy at the time but afterwards it can make you feel extremely low.

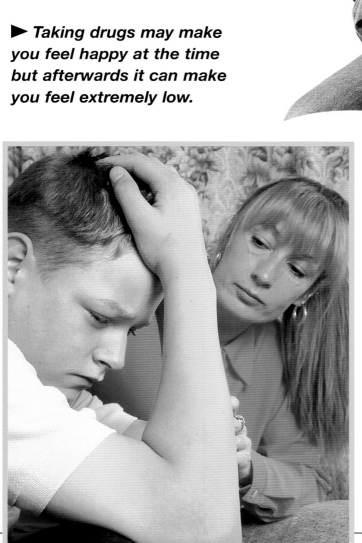

There are many organizations set up to help addicts recover from their addictions, but it is often very difficult for an addict to accept that they need help. Talking over the situation, discussing what went wrong and why, and taking everything one small step at a time can all help an addict to overcome their addiction and begin to lead a happy and healthy life again.

◄ If you are worried about a friend remember to talk to an adult.

How to keep safe

The most important thing you need to do as you grow up is to keep yourself safe. One of the ways to do this is to avoid harmful substances. The panel on page 26 suggests ways in which you can avoid substances you do not want to take. You can also keep yourself safe by avoiding places where you might be offered things. For example, if you know that a group of teenagers often hang around a particular street corner and smoke, then plan your route so that you don't have to go past them.

▲ *Stay away from people who use peer pressure to cause trouble.*

◀ *Being part of a group means that you should feel relaxed and be able to have fun with your friends.*

You can help to keep your brothers, sisters, friends and classmates safe too by being alert. Some of the signs that a person might be using a harmful substance include:

- sudden mood changes

- being sleepy and unable to concentrate

- being secretive and lying

- not being interested in things they usually liked, e.g. sport and other hobbies

- not taking as much care of themselves as they used to.

You should always tell an adult you trust if you think someone may have a substance problem. Do remember, though, all of these signs can also be just a perfectly normal part of growing up and do not necessarily mean that there is a problem.

▲ *Have fun without drugs.*

$\sim\!\!\sim$ Action Zone

If you suspect or know that someone close to you – a brother or sister, friend or classmate – has a substance problem, tell an adult you trust as soon as you can. You may think that this is 'telling tales', but it isn't. Anybody who has a substance problem needs help, and the sooner they get it, the sooner they can start to recover. By telling an adult about it, you are really beginning that recovery process for them.

▶ *Telling an adult can help to sort out a friend's problems.*

Glossary

addict a person who needs regular doses of a substance.

alcohol a drug that many people enjoy as a drink.

alcohol poisoning the result of too much alcohol in the blood for the body to cope.

anxious worrying about something.

blood vessels the tubes through which blood flows around the body.

crystalline looking like a crystal, a clear transparent mineral.

drug a substance that affects the body and how we feel.

hangover the after-effects of drinking too much alcohol.

irritates causes discomfort.

lungs the organs used for breathing.

medicine a drug that helps to cure an illness.

nausea a feeling of sickness.

nervous frightened or worried.

nicotine a chemical in tobacco that is very addictive.

passive smoking breathing in smoke from another person's cigarette.

responsible to be in control of.

solvent a chemical that gives off strong-smelling gases.

Other books to read

Alex Does Drugs by Janine Amos (Cherrytree Books, 2002)

We're Talking About Smoking by Karen Bryant (Hodder Wayland, 1995)

We're Talking About Drugs by Jenny Bryan (Hodder Wayland, 1995)

We're Talking About Alcohol by Jenny Bryan (Hodder Wayland, 1995)

What's at Issue - Drugs and You by Bridget Lawless (Heinemann, 2000)

Drugs And Your Health by Jillian Powell (Hodder Wayland, 1997)

Learn to Say No - Alcohol by Angela Royston (Heinemann, 2000)

Learn to Say No - Cannabis by Angela Royston (Heinemann, 2000)

Learn to Say No - Smoking by Angela Royston (Heinemann, 2000)

Learn to Say No - Solvents by Angela Royston (Heinemann, 2000)

Useful addresses

National Drugs Helpline

Tel: 0800 776600

Childline

Tel: 0800 1111

Lifeline

Tel: 0800 716701

Solvent Misuse Project

Tel: 020 843 6038

Index